SO-AXI-718

**The Cyrenius H. Booth Library
Newtown, Connecticut**

This Book the Gift of

Friends of the Library

Netherlands

by Sarah E. De Capua

Content Adviser: Meijken Engbers, M.S.,
Educational Geographer, Royal Netherlands Geography Association

Reading Adviser: Dr. Linda D. Labbo,
Department of Reading Education, College of Education,
The University of Georgia

COMPASS POINT BOOKS

Minneapolis, Minnesota

FIRST REPORTS

J
949.2
DEC
14.

Compass Point Books
3109 West 50th Street, #115
Minneapolis, MN 55410

Visit Compass Point Books on the Internet at *www.compasspointbooks.com*
or e-mail your request to *custserv@compasspointbooks.com*

Cover: A tour boat in an Amsterdam canal

Photographs ©: Dallas and John Heaton/Corbis, cover; Larry Lee Photography/Corbis, 4; Photo Network/Bill Terry, 6, 11; Dave Bartruff/Corbis, 7, 23; Bettmann/Corbis, 8–9; Hans Georg Roth/Corbis, 10; North Wind Picture Archives, 13; Hulton/Archive by Getty Images, 14, 15, 34, 36; Richard T. Nowitz/Corbis, 16; Julian Calder/Corbis, 17; Craig Lovell, 18; David L. Brown/Tom Stack & Associates, 19; Photo Network, 20; John Elk III, 21, 38–39; Jim Steinhart of www.PlanetWare.com, 22; Photo Network/Chad Ehlers, 24–25; Owen Franken/Corbis, 26, 40; Joe Viesti/The Viesti Collection, 27; Wiel Pelzer, 28; Michael Porro/Getty Images, 29; Reuters/Michael Kooren/Getty Images, 30–31; TRIP/A. Bloomfield, 32, 33; Bill Ross/Corbis, 35; Christian Sarramon/Corbis, 37; Michael DeFreitas, 42.

Editors: E. Russell Primm, Emily J. Dolbear, and Patricia Stockland
Photo Researcher: Svetlana Zhurkina
Photo Selector: Linda S. Koutris
Designer/Page Production: Bradfordesign, Inc./Biner Design
Cartographer: XNR Productions, Inc.

Library of Congress Cataloging-in-Publication Data
De Capua, Sarah.
 Netherlands / by Sarah De Capua.
  p. cm. — (First reports)
 Summary: Introduces the geography, history, culture, and people of the Netherlands, a small country in northern Europe. Includes bibliographical references and index.
 ISBN 0-7565-0426-0 (hardcover)
 1. Netherlands—History—Juvenile literature. 2. Netherlands—Social life and customs—Juvenile literature. [1. Netherlands.] I. Title. II. Series.
DJ18.D44 2003
949.2—dc21
                                                                      2002009929

© 2003 by Compass Point Books
All rights reserved. No part of this book may be reproduced without written permission from the publisher. The publisher takes no responsibility for the use of any of the materials or methods described in this book, nor for the products thereof.
Printed in the United States of America.

Table of Contents

NOTE: In this book, words that are defined in the glossary are
in **bold** the first time they appear in the text.

"Hallo!"

▲ *The Netherlands is famous for its windmills.*

"Hallo!" This is the Dutch way to greet someone. Dutch is the language of the Netherlands. The people of the Netherlands are called Dutch, too. The Netherlands is known for its windmills, tulips, and wooden shoes. The country is sometimes called Holland, but that's not its correct name.

The Netherlands is a small, flat country in northern Europe. It is a little larger than the U.S. state of Maryland. The Netherlands touches two countries. Germany lies to the east. Belgium is to the south.

▲ *Map of the Netherlands*

North and west of the country is the North Sea. Much of the Netherlands lies below **sea level.** However, the North Sea does not flood the land because the Dutch have built dikes, which are walls of dirt, to keep the water out.

△ *A beach along the North Sea*

▲ *The Peace Palace, the home of the Court of International Justice, is in The Hague.*

Amsterdam is the capital of the Netherlands. It is also the country's largest city. The central government is located in the city of The Hague. Other major cities include Rotterdam, Utrecht, and Maastricht.

Land and Weather

Long ago, the North Sea covered the low ground in the Netherlands. The Dutch built dikes and canals around the areas of water they wanted to drain. Then they used windmills to pump the water back into the sea.

All this work created large sections of dry land for people to live on and farm. Much of the Netherlands, then, is made up of land taken back from the sea. The Dutch still fight flooding of their land by the sea and rivers, however.

Four major rivers flow through the Netherlands. They are the Rhine, Maas, Schelde, and Waal. The Maas, Schelde, and Waal Rivers form a **delta** in the southern part of the country.

▲ *Workers building dikes in the Netherlands in 1953 to prevent flooding*

△ *The shoreline of one of the Wadden Islands*

Over time, sand from the sea has built up along the country's northern coast. These hills of sand are called dunes. They have formed the Wadden Islands.

The highest point in the country is Vaalser Berg. It is only 1,053 feet (321 meters) high. The country's lowest point is Prins Alexander Polder. It is 22 feet (7 meters) below sea level.

The weather in the Netherlands is wet and mild. Mild means it is not too hot or too cold. It does not snow much in winter. Fog and cloudy skies are common.

Summer is comfortable in the Netherlands. The skies are sunny. Warm breezes come off the ocean. Sudden rain showers may occur, though.

▲ *Fishing in the Netherlands*

History of the Netherlands

The earliest people to live in what is now the Netherlands arrived in the area around 4500 B.C. They came from central Europe and lived in villages. Over the next 3,000 years, other groups of people joined them.

About 300 B.C., tribes called the Germans and the Celts moved into an area called the Low Countries. This area included what are now the Netherlands, Belgium, and Luxembourg. The Germans lived in the north of the Low Countries. The Celts lived in the south.

After a while, a different tribe of Germans known as the Frisians moved into the northern area. In time, the Frisians moved south. Eventually, the Celts were pushed off the land.

Next, the Franks moved into the area and lived in the south. Today's Dutch language is based on the

▲ *The Franks moved into the Netherlands around* A.D. *300.*

language of the Franks. The Frisians had already moved to the seashore and the islands off the coast. By the A.D. 500s, they had become great sea traders.

From the 1100s to the 1500s, the Netherlands was part of different European kingdoms. In the late 1560s, Philip II of Spain ruled the Netherlands. He was not a wise ruler.

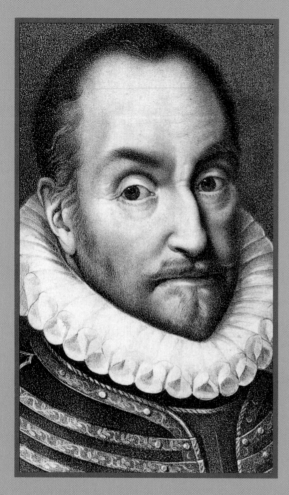

Willem I, Prince of Orange, leader of the Dutch rebels who wanted their independence from Spanish rule

In 1568, the Dutch fought back. They were led by Willem I, Prince of Orange. This was the beginning of the Eighty Years' War of Independence. The war ended in 1648 when the Netherlands won its freedom from Spain.

The Dutch were independent for nearly 150 years. Then in 1795, the French occupied the Netherlands. In 1814, French rule ended and the Kingdom of the Netherlands was created. The kingdom was first ruled by King Willem I. He was related to Willem I, Prince of Orange.

In 1940, World War II (1939–1945) was being fought. That year, Germany invaded the Netherlands. Germany controlled the Netherlands until the war ended in 1945. After the war, the Netherlands went back to being an independent kingdom.

▲ *German troops entering the Netherlands in 1940*

Today, the Kingdom of the Netherlands is still a **constitutional monarchy.** Queen Beatrix is the head of state. The prime minister, however, is the real head of government. The prime minister runs the country's day-to-day business and chooses members of a cabinet. A cabinet is a group of advisers.

The Netherlands has a **parliament.** All the members of parliament are elected by the people. Together, the prime minister, cabinet, and parliament run the country.

▲ *A national monument and the Royal Palace in Amsterdam*

Made in the Netherlands

The Dutch have always made a living from buying and selling goods to other countries. Rotterdam is the busiest **seaport** in the world. Every day, ships load and unload their cargo there.

▲ *Cargo ships at the busy seaport of Rotterdam*

Major **industries** exist in the Netherlands. Natural gas and petroleum are important industries. In fact, the Netherlands supplies most of Europe's natural gas. Food processing and metalworking are other important industries. About one in five people work in these and other manufacturing jobs.

Most Dutch people work in service industries. They are employed in places such as shops, banks, law firms, and government offices.

▲ *A shop owner prepares olives for sale in his Amsterdam deli.*

The Netherlands does not have a lot of farm-land. This is partly because of the country's small size. The land that is available, how-ever, is very productive. The combina-tion of the rich soil and the weather makes

▲ *Dutch farmland is very productive.*

the Netherlands a great place for farming.

There are small farms throughout the country. Sugar beets, potatoes, wheat, and barley are grown on these farms. Greenhouses can also be found out-side cities. Lettuce, tomatoes, cucumbers, grapes, and flowers grow well in these greenhouses.

Some of the world's best cheese is produced on the country's dairy farms and in factories. Gouda and Edam are the best-known Dutch cheeses.

⛰ *A cheese market in the Netherlands*

▲ *Tulips are among the country's most famous products.*

The Netherlands is famous for its tulips. Millions of tulips grow in rows as far as you can see. These colorful flowers are shipped all over the world.

Life in the Netherlands

▲ *Houseboats are not unusual homes for the Dutch.*

Most Dutch people live in towns and cities. Only a few people live in the countryside. Some Dutch people live on houseboats along the rivers. In towns and cities, many families live in apartments.

Houses are usually tall and narrow. Steep stair-cases can be found inside. Houses all over the country have large windows. Most also have gardens.

Dutch children between the ages of four and eighteen must attend school. Primary schools are for children ages four to twelve. They learn reading, writing, mathematics, history, science, and social studies. In their final two years, they learn English.

After age twelve, students attend secondary school. Secondary school prepares students to attend college or go to work.

▲ *Dutch students wear traditional dress for a field trip to a museum.*

After school and work, the Dutch have time to relax. Family life is important to the Dutch. Many Dutch families like to stay home. They play games, talk, watch television, or read books.

Some young people like to visit friends or ride their bicycles in the evenings. Adults read the newspaper, take walks, or invite friends to their homes.

Many Dutch enjoy sports. *Voetbal* is the national sport of the Netherlands. Voetbal is known as soccer in the United States and Canada. Tennis is another popular sport in the Netherlands.

In summer, the Dutch enjoy swimming, sailing, field hockey, and biking. Bicycling is also a regular form

of transportation. Most children walk or bike to school each day. Many adults ride bikes to work, to visit friends, and to do errands.

▲ *Taking bike and pony rides is a fun way for children in the Netherlands to spend their time outside of school.*

In winter, ice-skating is the most popular activity. When it is cold enough to freeze the canals, the Dutch skate on them. Speed skating and figure skating are common winter sports.

△ *Frozen canals in the Netherlands make good ice-skating rinks.*

Holidays and Festivals

▲ *Sinterklaas gives presents on December 5.*

The Dutch have a variety of holidays and festivals.
Some are religious. Others reflect the Dutch culture.

On December 5, they celebrate St. Nicholas's Eve,
which is the Dutch Christmas. St. Nicholas is called
Sinterklaas. He has a helper named Zwarte Piet. Everyone gives and receives presents on St. Nicholas's Eve.

New Year's Eve is also a time for celebrating. Church bells ring. Fireworks are set off. People gather together to welcome the new year.

In the southern region of the Netherlands, Carnival Day is celebrated in February or March. Carnival Day marks the start of **Lent.** People enjoy music, dances, and parades.

▲ *A group in Kerkrade dresses as the elements of gold, silver, and bronze during Carnival. Colors, fun, and music are always part of the Carnival celebration.*

In spring, the Dutch celebrate Easter. Children hunt for decorated eggs. "Easter men" made of bread are a special treat.

On April 30, the Dutch observe the most important national holiday—Queen's Day. It is the day the queen's birthday is celebrated. Towns and cities are decorated with colorful balloons, lights, and flags. Everyone gets the day off from work or school to honor the queen.

The second Saturday in May is National Windmill Day. On that day, all of the windmills in the country are

▲ Queen Beatrix celebrates her birthday on Queen's Day, which is actually the birthday of her mother, Princess Juliana.

opened to the public. Some people take tours through the windmills. It is a day to celebrate one of the country's national **symbols.**

Each June and July, the Holland Festival is held. Plays, concerts, dances, and exhibits draw people to the country from all over Europe.

The North Sea Jazz Festival is held in The Hague every July. It features jazz musicians and bands. The city of Utrecht also hosts a music festival.

▲ *About 470 dress shirts are hung out in the sun as part of the Oerol theater festival. Blowing in the wind, the shirts look like clouds hanging over the beach.*

Children riding a float decorated with flowers

Flower festivals are popular in the Netherlands. They are held in towns and cities all over the country. These festivals usually take place in August and September. They feature parades with floats and marching bands. The floats are decorated with thousands of flowers.

The Hague also holds a fireworks festival every August. Crafts festivals and horse fairs are held in different regions of the country.

Arts and Literature

The Dutch have a history of great musicians and artists. Dutch architecture and filmmaking are also well respected.

The Dutch enjoy all kinds of music. Their tastes include classical, jazz, popular, and folk. At least one person in nearly every family plays an instrument. Some people enjoy singing in choirs as well.

◄ *A guitar player and a street performer in Amsterdam*

Some of the world's most famous artists were Dutch. The works of Rembrandt van Rijn, Vincent van Gogh, and Johannes Vermeer hang in museums throughout the world.

Architecture is the art of designing and building structures. Dutch architecture is world famous.

△ *Rembrandt van Rijn*

The homes built along Amsterdam's canals are only three windows wide. These houses are tall and deep. They were built this way because of the lack of space for home building. They are known for their gables. Gables are parts of a roof, and they come in different forms. Some look like steps. Others are shaped like bells or triangles. Some are plain. Others have decorations cut into them.

Not all Dutch buildings are built in this traditional style. Rem Koolhaas is a famous modern Dutch architect. He has designed many buildings in the Netherlands and other countries.

▲ *Houses in Amsterdam are often narrow and have decorative gables.*

Harry Mulisch is a famous Dutch novelist.

Many movies from the Netherlands have won important awards. *Antonia's Line* and *Character*, for example, won Academy Awards in the 1990s.

The Netherlands has a history of famous authors and poets. In 1788, Elizabeth Bekker-Wolff and Agatha Deken wrote one of the country's earliest novels. Multatuli wrote important works in the 1800s.

In recent history, Willem Hermans, Harry Mulisch, Gerard Reve, and Jan Wolkers have written stories that became known throughout the world. Simon Vestdijk's works have been translated into several languages. Famous Dutch poets include Willem Bilderdijk, Dirk Coster, and Hendrik Marsman.

Traditional crafts have a special place in the country's society. Pottery, colorful tiles, baskets, and clocks are all well-known Dutch creations. Delftware is the blue and white pottery made in Delft. Two factories still produce Delftware using 300-year-old methods such as a pottery wheel and hand-painted designs. In some towns, craftspeople can be found carving wooden shoes or making leather goods.

◀ *Delft pottery on sale in Zaanse Schans*

Dutch Food

Dutch food is plain but delicious. Meals include bread, fruits, vegetables, and dairy products. The country's position next to the North Sea means there is plenty of seafood, too. The Dutch especially enjoy herring, which is eaten raw. Salmon, shrimp, and mussels are also popular.

For breakfast, Dutch people usually eat bread with different toppings. Favorite toppings include butter, jelly, meat, or cheese. Sometimes people have a boiled egg with breakfast.

Lunch is similar to breakfast. Sometimes people eat a sandwich of buttered bread with bacon or ham, topped with two fried eggs.

This is called an *uitsmijter* (OUTS-may-ter). Soup is sometimes eaten at lunchtime.

For most Dutch, supper is the main meal of the day. The meal starts with thick soup. This is followed by fish or meat, potatoes, and vegetables.

▲ *Bread, boiled eggs, meat, and cheese are part of a typical Dutch breakfast.*

Desserts are usually simple. They include fruit, ice cream, fruit pies, and puddings.

Large pancakes served with apples, bacon, or sugar beet syrup are popular, too. A Dutch favorite is *poffertjes* (POF-er-tches). They are small, round pancakes. Poffertjes have no filling. Instead, they are sprinkled with sugar.

△ *When these poffertjes are cooked, they will be sprinkled with sugar.*

Dutch Clothing

Dutch people dress the way people in the United States and Canada do. Black, gray, and brown are the usual colors for clothing. Businesspeople wear suits. Young people like to wear jeans and T-shirts.

Like people from many other cultures, the Dutch used to have their own style of clothing. The men wore black jackets and loose pants. Their hats had wide brims. The women wore long, colorful dresses. Lace bonnets or caps covered their heads. Some women wore hats that covered their ears. Others wore pointed hats with ends that curled next to each ear. Children's clothing was similar to these adult styles. It was more colorful, though.

Many Dutch people wore wooden shoes. Those are not very common today. Some Dutch, however, wear them when they are farming, fishing, or gardening. The shoes keep their feet dry. Today, wooden shoes are sold mostly to visitors from other countries.

Few Dutch people still wear traditional clothes. Those who do live in a few small villages. Other people wear them only at festivals or during holidays.

These girls wear the pointed hats and wooden shoes that used to be part of standard Dutch clothing.

The Netherlands Today

▲ *A street artist dressed as a knight shakes hands with young tourists in Amsterdam.*

The Netherlands is a small country, but its people have been very successful. Visitors from all over the world go to the Netherlands. They go to see the tulips and windmills. They also visit museums and historic places. All of this helps them to experience the rich culture and traditions of the Netherlands.

Glossary

constitutional monarchy—a country ruled by a king or queen in which the ruler has only those powers given by the nation's constitution and laws

delta—an area of land shaped like a fan where a river enters the sea

industries—manufacturing companies and other businesses

Lent—the forty days before Easter, not including Sundays, in the Christian Church's year

parliament—a group of people who are elected to make laws

sea level—the surface of the ocean, used as a starting point from which to measure the height or depth of a place

seaport—a town or city on the seacoast with a harbor where ships can dock and load or unload cargo

symbols—objects that represent something else

Did You Know?

- The Dutch name for the Netherlands is *Nederland.* This means "low land."

- The Kingdom of the Netherlands includes the islands of Aruba and the Netherlands Antilles, located in the Caribbean Sea.

- The Dutch name Sinterklaas became Santa Claus in English.

- Wooden shoes are called *klompen* in Dutch.

- Orange is the national color of the Netherlands. It honors Willem I, Prince of Orange, and the royal family. On Queen's Day, everyone wears orange.

At a Glance

Official name: Kingdom of the Netherlands

Capital: Amsterdam

Official language: Dutch

National song: "Wilhelmus van Nassouwe" ("William of Nassau")

Area: 16,036 square miles (41,533 square kilometers)

Highest point: Vaalser Berg at 1,053 feet (321 meters)

Lowest point: Prins Alexander Polder at 22 feet (7 meters) below sea level

Population: 16,067,754 (2002 estimate)

Head of government: Prime minister

Money: Euro

Important Dates

4500 B.C.	The earliest people in the present-day Netherlands move into the area from central Europe.
300 B.C.	The Germans and the Celts move into the area.
A.D. 500s	After being pushed out of the area by the Franks, the Frisians become great sea traders.
1100–1500	The Netherlands is part of various European kingdoms.
1560s	Philip II of Spain rules the Netherlands.
1568	Willem I, Prince of Orange, leads a rebellion, and the Eighty Years' War of Independence begins.
1648	The Netherlands wins its independence from Spain.
1795	France occupies the Netherlands.
1814	The present-day Kingdom of the Netherlands is created.
1940	Germany invades the Netherlands during World War II.
1945	World War II ends with Germany's defeat, and the Netherlands is an independent kingdom again.
2002	The euro replaces the guilder as the currency in the Netherlands.

Want to Know More?

At the Library

Britton, Tamara L. *The Netherlands.* Edina, Minn.: Abdo & Daughters, 2002.

Reynolds, Simon. *Welcome to the Netherlands.* Milwaukee: Gareth Stevens, 2002.

van Fenema, Joyce. *The Netherlands.* Milwaukee: Gareth Stevens, 1998.

On the Web

Infoplease.com—The Netherlands
http://www.infoplease.com/ipa
For basic facts about the Dutch language, population, and history

The Netherlands Board of Tourism
http://www.holland.com
For photographs and information about the country's history and attractions

The Netherlands—Travel for Kids
http://www.travelforkids.com/Funtodo/Netherlands
For profiles of activities and attractions for families visiting Amsterdam and the Netherlands

Through the Mail

The Royal Netherlands Embassy
4200 Linnean Avenue, N.W.
Washington, DC 20008
202/244-5300
To learn more about the Netherlands and to plan a trip

On the Road

Tulip Time Festival
http://www.tuliptime.org/
To find out more about visiting Holland, Michigan, during its famous May tulip festival

About the Author

Sarah E. De Capua enjoys writing about other countries. Researching the manuscripts gives her a chance to read many other books about those countries. Reading good books about faraway places can be a way to visit them!

When she is not working as an author and editor of children's books, De Capua enjoys traveling from her home in Colorado to places she has written about as well as to places she may write about in the future.